KT-130-656

430408

MESS

THE MANUAL OF
ACCIDENTS AND
MISTAKES

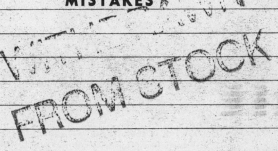
WITHDRAWN FROM STOCK

Keri Smith

PENGUIN BOOKS

PENGUIN BOOKS

Published by the Penguin Group
Penguin Books Ltd, 80 Strand, London WC2R ORL, England
Penguin Group (USA) Inc., 375 Hudson Street, New York, New York 10014, USA
Penguin Group (Canada), 90 Eglinton Avenue East, Suite 700, Toronto, Ontario, Canada M4P 2Y3
(a division of Pearson Penguin Canada Inc.)
Penguin Ireland, 25 St Stephen's Green, Dublin 2, Ireland (a division of Penguin Books Ltd)
Penguin Group (Australia), 250 Camberwell Road, Camberwell, Victoria 3124, Australia
(a division of Pearson Australia Group Pty Ltd)
Penguin Books India Pvt Ltd, 11 Community Centre, Panchsheel Park, New Delhi – 110 017, India
Penguin Group (NZ), 67 Apollo Drive, Rosedale, North Shore 0632, New Zealand
(a division of Pearson New Zealand Ltd)
Penguin Books (South Africa) (Pty) Ltd, 24 Sturdee Avenue, Rosebank,
Johannesburg 2196, South Africa

Penguin Books Ltd, Registered Offices: 80 Strand, London WC2R ORL, England

www.penguin.com

First published in the USA by Penguin Group (USA) Inc., 2010
First published in Great Britain by Penguin Books 2010

014

Copyright © Keri Smith, 2010
All rights reserved

The moral right of the author has been asserted

Printed in Great Britain by Clays Ltd, St Ives plc

Except in the United States of America, this book is sold subject
to the condition that it shall not, by way of trade or otherwise, be lent,
re-sold, hired out, or otherwise circulated without the publisher's
prior consent in any form of binding or cover other than that in
which it is published and without a similar condition including this
condition being imposed on the subsequent purchaser

978-1-846-14447-9

www.greenpenguin.co.uk

MIX
Paper from
responsible sources
FSC™ C018179
FSC
www.fsc.org

Penguin Books is committed to a sustainable
future for our business, our readers and our planet.
This book is made from Forest Stewardship
Council™ certified paper.

153.
35
SMI

WARNING:

DO NOT TRY TO MAKE SOMETHING BEAUTIFUL. DO NOT THROW THIS BOOK OUT WHEN YOU DISLIKE A PAGE YOU CREATED. DO NOT PLAY IT SAFE. DO NOT WORRY ABOUT LEGIBILITY. DO HAVE FUN. DO GET DIRTY. DO TRY SOMETHING YOU'VE NEVER TRIED BEFORE. DON'T THINK TOO MUCH. (IT ALWAYS HELPS TO QUIET THE MIND.)

WRITE YOUR OWN INTRO ↓

Note: You may choose to read the following eight-page introduction, or you can choose to skip it and write your own version in the space on the left. You may also wish to begin the exercises immediately.

INTRODUCTION

A few years ago I became fascinated by the work of Dutch-born artist Bas Jan Ader. The first piece I saw of his was the video "Broken Fall," which depicts a man hanging precariously by his hands from a high tree branch, swinging back and forth over a small creek. As the branch bobs and sways, I found myself waiting for the inevitable. Amid the tension of waiting, I also found myself smiling and laughing uncontrollably. And then it happens. The man plunges into the creek and crawls up the side of the bank, the whole thing lasting a mere 1 minute, 44 seconds.

Ader often dealt with the subject of gravity—various methods of falling, or dropping things. It seems completely ridiculous, and this is what I love about it. It is absurd, brilliantly simple, and completely serious at the same time.

In the film, there is an interview with an old Dutch sailor that sums up Ader's work perfectly. He speaks indirectly about the process of improvisation, but the connection I made from it is that the point of Ader's "falls" is not the falling but the moment (1/10th of a second) where he makes the decision to let go. That is the moment of transcendence when you leave everything behind and leap into the unknown.

As improvisers, artists, or experimenters, we are trying to re-create that moment–when you leave everything behind and leap into the unknown. Because we've done it before and it's addictive–that seductive release, a sense of giddyness mixed with fear. For an instant you get a feeling that you are really doing something worthwhile, living out on the edge of something big, yet unnamable. A kind of opening (with all the vulnerability that comes with that).

We all know what it feels like to fall, but how many of us have experimented with gravity as a medium? Isn't falling or breaking things something we only do by accident? What does it feel like to throw yourself off balance on purpose?

Definition of "mistake" or "accident" (for the purposes of this book): *Happenings or occurrences by which the creator does not have complete control over the final outcome (end result) that result in conclusions the creator did not predict. We might also call them "experiments."*

During the course of working on this book, I realized that what I am really talking about when I speak of "mistakes" is improvisation. The process of improvising involves throwing ourselves off balance for a time, into a situation where we have to make decisions on the spot. Forced decision making puts us into a place where we have no choice but to accept what has occurred and then move on, to work with what exists. But it also pushes us into some places that we would not normally go. This to me is the purpose of this book: to participate in some situations where you have limited control and venture into territory that you would not normally go with the possibility of creating something completely new and different than what you might have done before.

DEREK BAILEY ON IMPROVISATION:

"A LOT OF IMPROVISERS FIND IMPROVISATION WORTHWHILE, I THINK, BECAUSE OF THE POSSIBILITIES. THINGS THAT CAN HAPPEN BUT PERHAPS RARELY DO. ONE OF THOSE THINGS IS THAT YOU ARE 'TAKEN OUT OF YOURSELF.' SOMETHING HAPPENS WHICH SO DISORIENTATES YOU THAT, FOR A TIME, WHICH MIGHT ONLY LAST A SECOND OR TWO, YOUR REACTIONS AND RESPONSES ARE NOT WHAT THEY NORMALLY WOULD BE. YOU CAN DO SOMETHING YOU DIDN'T REALIZE YOU WERE CAPABLE OF."

One of the biggest handicaps that occurs with both trained and untrained artists is a kind of reverential attitude toward making things "beautiful, accurate, and perfect." What is missing in this approach is a spontaneity or playful attitude with regard to materials and process. There is a lack of experimentation. In this approach the final product becomes more important than the process.

With the exercises in this book I would like to propose partaking in the experience and process of creating something with a total disregard of the outcome. Let's make the experience the thing. What if you were completely liberated from the final product?

SO, HOW DO YOU MAKE A MISTAKE ON PURPOSE?

It is my hope that by opening oneself up to the unknown at first in small ways (such as playing with materials), we begin to create a "habit" of experimentation. Slowly we become more accustomed to taking risks with our work. In time this can translate into bigger steps, both with creating a piece of artwork and in life. In this sense, whether it is really a mistake or not is irrelevant.

WHY WOULD YOU WANT TO DO THIS?

Contemplating and actively participating in imperfection (occasions where we open to failure) brings to us a freedom because it allows us to relax and enjoy the ebb and flow of life. Life does not always bring to us things that are "tidy." There is beauty to be found in the mess.

Messes can also be beneficial in presenting unexpected connections and juxtapositions. These often lead to new ideas, explorations, combinations, and solutions.

DON'T CLEAN YOUR DESK. YOU MIGHT FIND SOMETHING IN THE MORNING THAT YOU CAN'T SEE TONIGHT.
— BRUCE MAU

MISTAKES AND MESSES IN DIFFERENT CONTEXTS (WAYS OF APPROACHING IMPROVISATION):

-movement (getting lost, tripping, walking backwards, throwing)
-materials (cutting, dripping, dropping, crushing, decaying, etc.)
-writing (abolishing grammar and spelling)
-social interactions (speech, actions)

TECHNIQUES YOU WILL USE IN THIS BOOK

-serendipity (the effect by which one accidentally discovers something fortunate, especially while looking for something entirely unrelated)
-indeterminacy (work created using chance, luck, or magic)
-scarcity/excess of material
-improvisation/intuition
-play, exploring the qualities of materials
-deviance (straying from norms)
-misinterpretation
-interruptions, participating in an activity and seeing what happens when it is interrupted at different points (interruption methods can be random or planned)
-combining new ideas
-speed
-underestimation and overestimation
-subconscious thought
-détournement, a concept created by the Situationists, which is an alteration to an existing work that gives it a new meaning.

METHOD

The following exercises are designed to do two things:

1. To throw you into a place where you have little or no control over the outcome.
2. To work with a variety of materials in an exploratory fashion.

MATERIALS YOU MAY NEED:

scissors, pen, pencil, ink, water, some kind of water-based paint, charcoal, sticks, white glue, tape, crayons, paper, coffee, tea, juice, ice cream, sand paper, shovel, chalk, dictionary, stones, found photo, magazine or newspaper, paper bag, straw, elastic band, markers, bowl, pushpins, leaves, balloons, food, dirt, can, egg carton, toilet paper roll, plastic bags, cereal box, fabric, blue things, string, hammer, chalk, egg, paintbrush, cardboard, an eraser, a digital camera, a coin, dust, cocoa, flour, pin, iron, ash, gumption.

There is no such thing
as a failed experiment,
only experiments with
unexpected outcomes.

–R. Buckminster Fuller

AND SO WE BEGIN...

1. While drawing a line, have someone bump this book.
2. Repeat numerous times.
Alternate: Draw a line while you are on the subway, in a car,
on the bus, etc. Take notes on date, time, location.

1. Cover this page with something sticky (glue, honey, etc.).
2. Drop a powdery substance onto the page (cocoa, flour, etc.).
3. Blow off excess.

Drop some kind of colored liquid (ink, tea, coffee) here from a good height (at least five feet).

HERE IS MUCH BEAUTY TO BE FOUND IN DRIPS AND SPLOTCHES.

DO NOT STICK ANYTHING HERE. DO NOT SCRIBBLE ON THIS PAGE. DO NOT COVER UP THIS TYPE. DO NOT TOUCH THIS PAGE WITH DIRTY HANDS. DO NOT READ THIS PAGE WHILE EATING. DO NOT WALK ON THIS PAGE WITH YOUR SHOES. DO NOT RUB THIS PAGE WITH DIRT. DO NOT FOLD DOWN THE CORNERS OF THIS PAGE. DO NOT WRITE NOTES TO YOUR FRIENDS HERE. DO NOT TEAR THIS PAGE. DO NOT GET THIS PAGE WET. DO NOT LET A FRIEND WRITE ON THIS PAGE. DO NOT TRY TO COVER UP THIS PAGE.

Break the rules.

1. Rub some kind of pigment on your elbows (dirt, paint, ash, etc.).
2. Lean here.

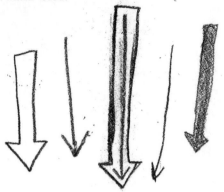

1. Cut pieces of white paper into tiny strips (1/8 inch
   X 1 inch).
2. Coat black page with white glue.
3. Drop the strips one at a time from a good height.
4. Press the strips down where they landed so they stick
   to the page.

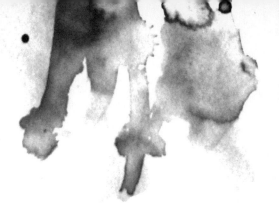

1. Drip some kind of colored liquid here (ink, watercolor, tea, juice, etc.).
2. Move the book so that it runs in all directions.
3. Let dry.
Alternate: Blow liquid with a straw (see image on last page), or fold page to create a symmetrical inkblot.

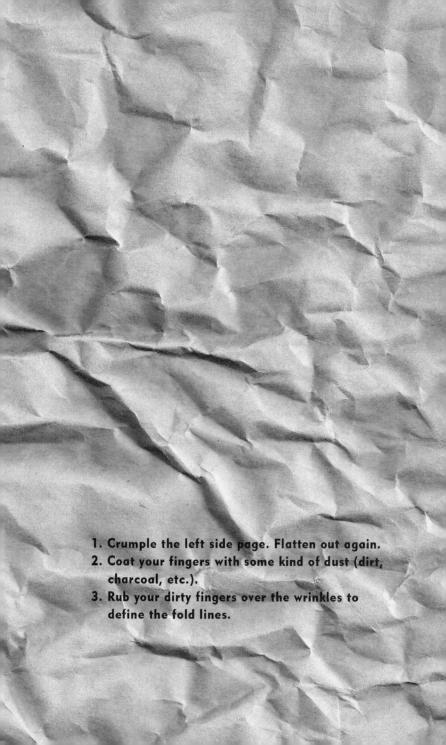

1. Crumple the left side page. Flatten out again.
2. Coat your fingers with some kind of dust (dirt, charcoal, etc.).
3. Rub your dirty fingers over the wrinkles to define the fold lines.

1. Do a painting in a water-based medium (pen, marker, watercolor, etc.).
2. Leave it out during a rain or snowstorm.

1. Alter this image by damaging it.
2. Find an interesting way to repair the damage.

FURTHER
RESEARCH:
BORO TEXTILES
OF JAPAN

Re-create these lines.

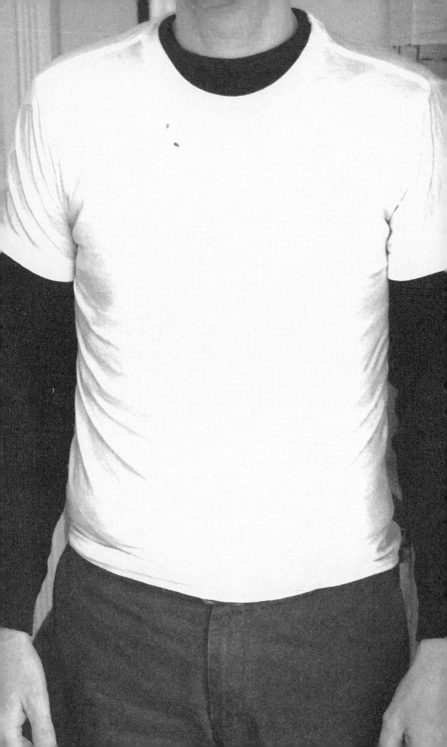

Mess up this shirt.
Some ideas: Crack an egg, wipe it off.
Splatter something. Drip ink. Doodle.

FURTHER RESEARCH:
JACKSON POLLOCK

Splatter, drip, and fling.

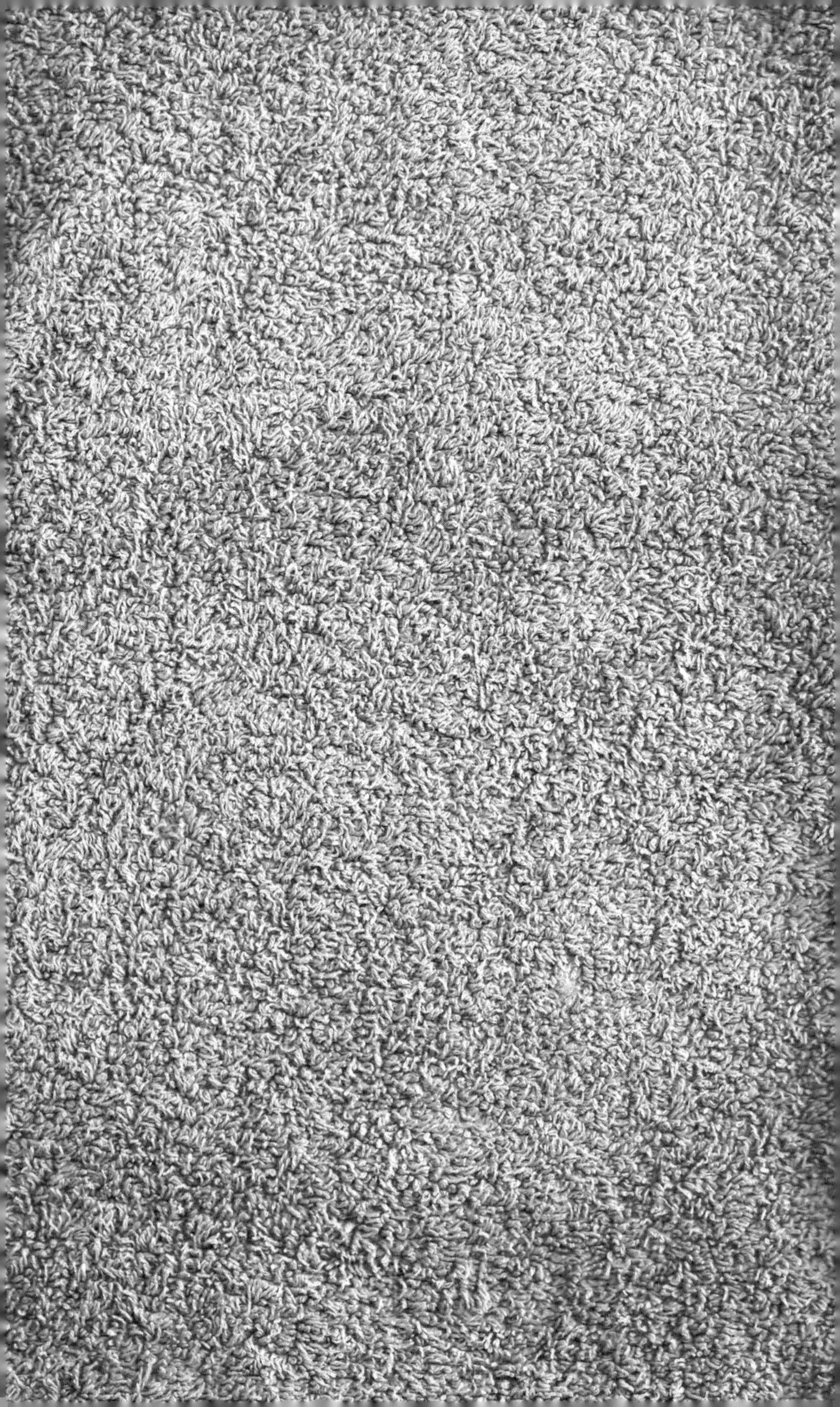

1. Spill something onto your hand or face (ice cream, glue, etc.).
2. Use this space to remove the excess.

1. Take a couple of crayons.
2. Scrape the crayons with a knife to create shavings. Place shavings in middle of the left-hand page.
3. Fold the page in half.
4. Using an iron on a low setting, go over the folded page with a few quick passes until the wax melts.
5. Open page to reveal design.

1. Cut a shape out of cardboard to use as a stencil.

2. Drop the shape onto the page.

3. Paint or color around the shape.

4. Repeat.

CHARCOAL
WITH FINGER
SMUDGE

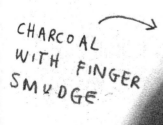

DISASTER AREA

This is a disaster area. Fill every square inch of this page with stuff.

For an entire day do all of your necessary tasks using your "wrong" hand. Record your exploits here (using your "wrong" hand).

Make a mess quickly without thinking. In one minute you must do ten different things to this page (i.e., break, stretch, tear, crush, fold). Ready. GO!

Add some harsh weather to this page (fog, snow, rain, etc.).

1. Soak this page with water.
2. Try to write on it.
Alternate: Drop ink onto wet page.

Create a tangle using some kind of
string-like material. Affix it here.

Take an existing mess (spill, etc.) and find a way to amplify it. Make it bigger. Exaggerate it.

PERFECT

Alter this image by using a variety of techniques (e.g., scrubbing, tearing, sanding, etc.).

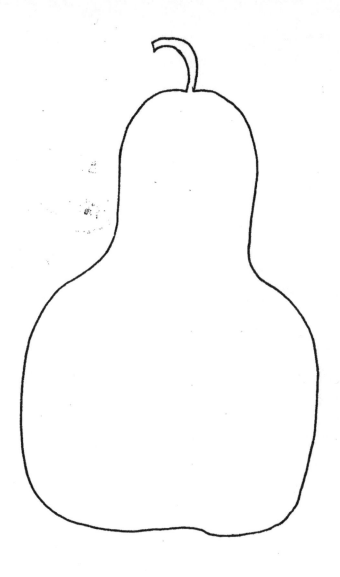

Color this in with your eyes closed (or in the dark).

1. Bury this book.
2. After three days, dig it up.

Try these various smudging techniques. With a wet medium (paint): drag an object over it (squeegee-like), blot with another piece of paper, drip water over top, blow. With a dry medium (pencil): rub with your finger, use some kind of solvent (water, alcohol), drag along the ground. Experiment with as many different materials as you can.

← **1. Do a drawing or painting here.**
2. After seven days, destroy it.

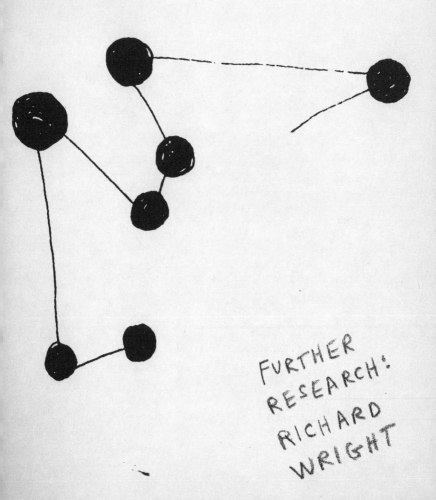

FURTHER
RESEARCH:
RICHARD
WRIGHT

1. Apply a horizontal line of white glue to the top of this page.
2. Support the book somehow so the paint runs down the page as it dries.
3. Once it is dry, add a coat of ink or paint overtop. Let dry.
4. Sand the page slightly to bring out the glue shapes.

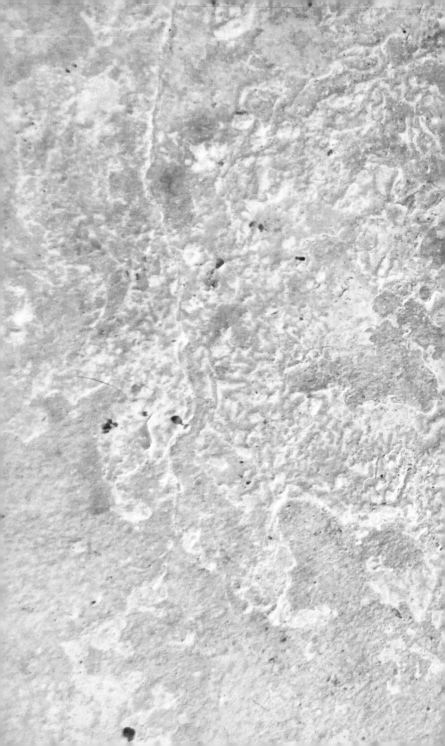

1. Get a hammer.
2. Take a drawing device such as a piece of chalk, charcoal, crayon, pencil, etc.
3. Smash.
4. Repeat.

1. Find a long stick.
2. Tape a pen to the end of it.
3. Try to draw something holding the far end of the stick.

Draw the sun using ten different methods.

FURTHER RESEARCH: BRUNO MUNARI

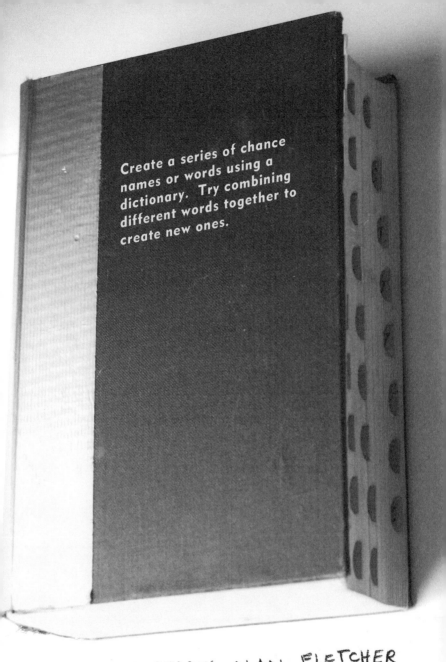

Create a series of chance names or words using a dictionary. Try combining different words together to create new ones.

FURTHER RESEARCH: ALAN FLETCHER

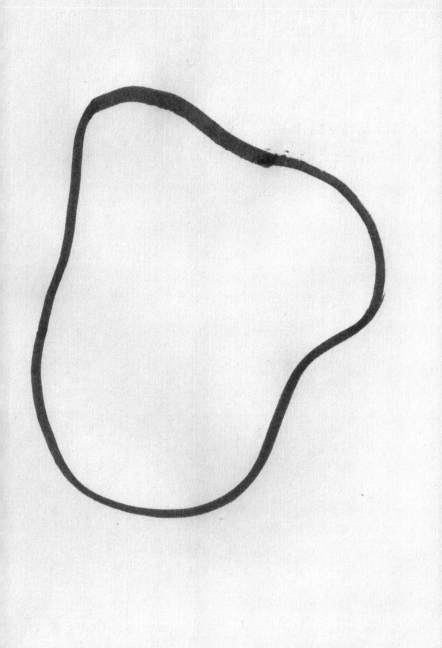

Trace this line as fast as you can for several minutes.

PUBLIC MESS

Create a small mess out in public.
Leave it for someone else to find.
Encourage others to add to it.
(Ideas: pile of stones, series of lines,
a drawing, a footprint, etc.)

1. Drop an amount of ink onto a page to create a random blob.
2. Create a character out of it.
3. Repeat.

This man looks like he needs to let loose a little. You might want to help him out. A new hat, some glasses, facial hair perhaps?

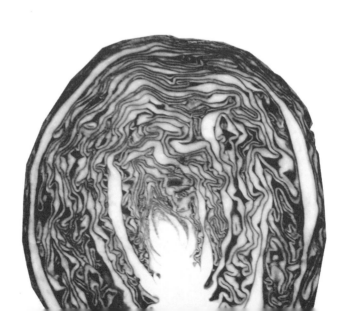

Continue this picture.

SOMETIMES IT IS GOOD TO PLAY WITH YOUR FOOD.

Abrasion test. Sand this image until it is gone.

FURTHER RESEARCH: FLUXUS

Create a series of thumbprints as the basis for drawing other objects (i.e., doodle over top of them). Also try working with handprints.

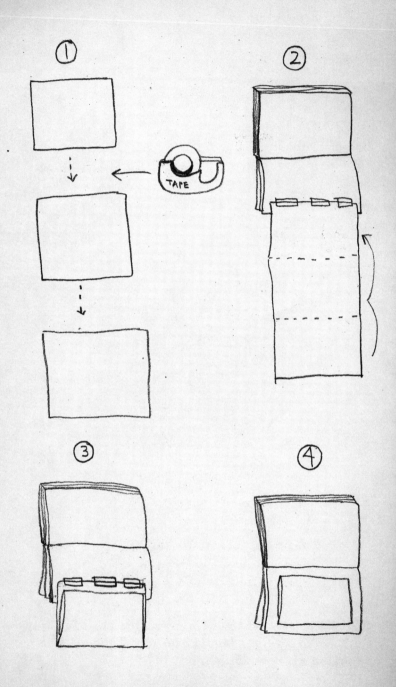

① ② ③ ④

TAPE

1. Create an extra-long page by taping a few extra sheets of paper to this page.
2. Create a spill (so that it looks like it is spilling out onto the floor).

1. Scratch on the black page (create a
   series of different textures).
2. Cut out some shapes.
3. Make a five-minute collage.

1. Find a magazine.
2. Turn to page 32.
3. If there is a photo on that page cut it out.
   (If there is no photo, try page 50.)
4. Make connections between yourself and the
   image in as many ways as possible.

Alternate: Acquire a photo of someone else's
family.

ON A JOURNEY
NO MATTER WHERE.
– HERMANN HESSE

FIELD TRIP

1. Go on an adventure with no money.
2. Document it here.

RECIPE:

AMOUNT	INGREDIENTS	DIRECTIONS

Create your own recipe using only things you have in your fridge and cupboards. Attempt something you've never made before.

1. Start with a simple drawing (a shape, a word, a line).
2. Every day for one month add something to the page. Experiment with many different mediums and techniques. You can also experiment with erasing parts as well.
3. Document the process with photos. (If you wish you can put all the photos together to make a stop motion animation.)

FURTHER RESEARCH : JENNI ROPE

Fill in this five-inch square by using all of
the colors you have on hand.

FURTHER
RESEARCH:
SOL LEWITT

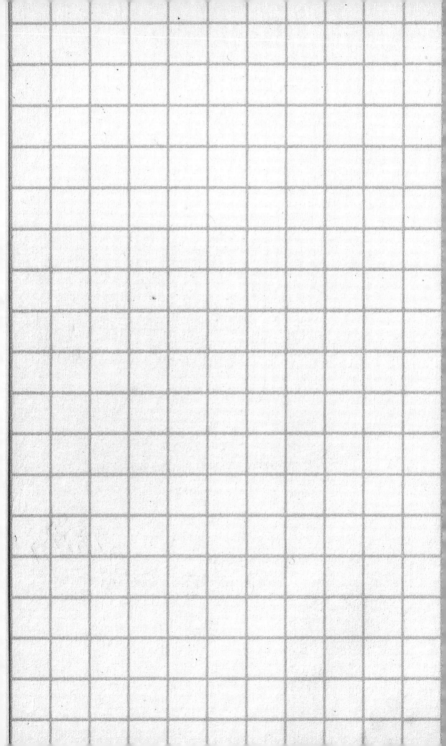

1. Select a series of ten colors in any medium.
2. Fill in each square in this grid in some kind of regular sequence.
3. Insert a mistake somewhere.

FURTHER
RESEARCH:
ANDRÉ
CADERE

1. Use this page to sweep up dirt in your room.
2. Find a way to contain the dirt here.
3. Use the dirt in an art piece.

EVERYBODY IS
BORN AN
INVENTOR.
— R. BUCKMINSTER
   FULLER

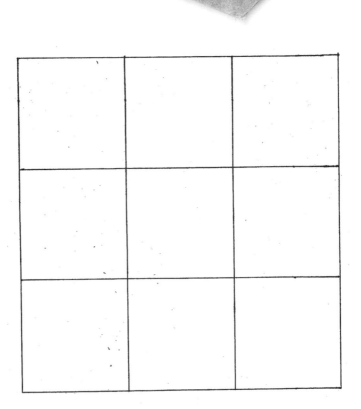

FURTHER
RESEARCH:
EVA HESSE

RANDOM SCULPTURE

1. On each of the squares write the name of an everyday object you have on hand. (Some ideas: paper, cardboard, can, egg carton, toilet paper roll, paper clips, string, twigs, rocks, plastic bags, cereal box, fabric, etc.)
2. Cut out the squares and put them in a hat. Pick three.
3. Create a sculpture using only what you have chosen.
4. Document it with a photo.

DÉTOURNEMENT

**Alter this image, or deface it to change the
meaning of it completely.**

photo credit: Ignoto

FURTHER
RESEARCH:
THE
SITUATIONIST
MOVEMENT

Fill this tree with interesting things.

DRAWING TO SOUNDS

In this exercise the sounds in your environment de-
termine what you draw. (Works best if you are in a
sound-intensive environment.) If you are hearing
many sounds at once you must pick one to draw to.

high-pitched sounds = circles
low-pitched sounds = straight lines
human voices = small dots
machine sounds = fast scribble
traffic sounds = lines that stop and start

Try using your hand as a writing instrument. Use whatever method possible.

A page to stick only blue things.

C5482282203

إلى

SUBCONSCIOUS MESS

1. Set out a bunch of supplies (pencils, paints, etc.). Write or draw without censoring.
2. Make a move solely by using your intuition.

RESEARCH:
AUTOMATIC WRITING
OR DRAWING USED
BY THE
SURREALISTS

THERE'S NOTHING
WE REALLY NEED
TO DO THAT
ISN'T DANGEROUS.
— JOHN CAGE

GROUP MESS

Start scribbling here (it has already been started for you).
Ask some friends to help you finish the whole page.

Take a series of blurry photos on purpose.

WRITING MESS

1. Write a sentence on each line.
2. Cut out strips.
3. Recombine sentences to create new poems.

Alternate:
1. Take a paragraph from one of your favorite writers.
2. Copy it here.
3. Cut it up.
4. Rearrange the words.

FURTHER RESEARCH:
RAYMOND QUENEAU
AND OULIPO

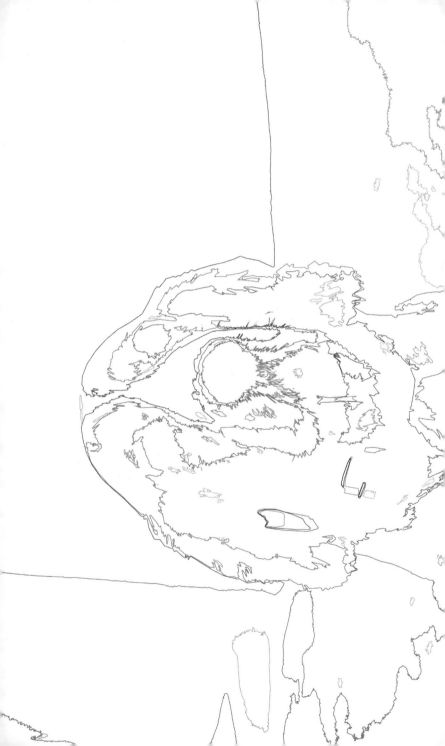

Fill in this paint-by-number using random colors.

Create a mess here with a friend while having lunch together.

SHORT ATTENTION SPAN PAGE

Do something in each square for only 10 seconds.

Lose your balance. Do something that throws you off-kilter. Attempt to record it in some way (photo, video, writing).

FURTHER RESEARCH: BAS JAN ADER

1. Take a magazine or a newspaper.
2. Cut a shape out of several layers.
3. Arrange the shapes into some configuration to make a collage.
4. Glue them down.

Alternate: Cover page with glue and drop the shapes, letting them stay where they land.

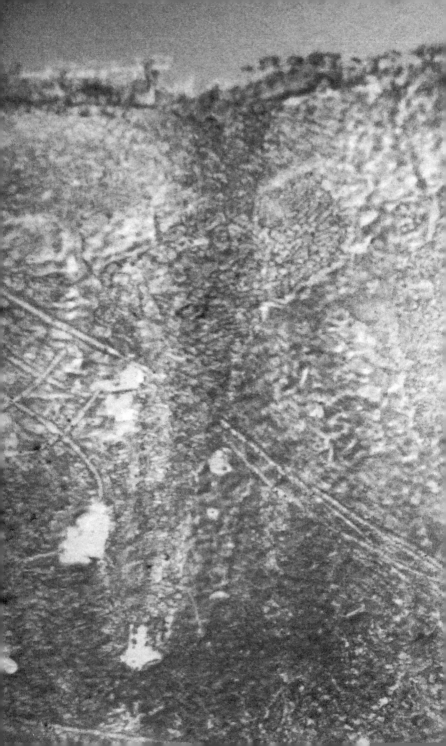

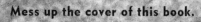

Mess up the cover of this book.
Do it!

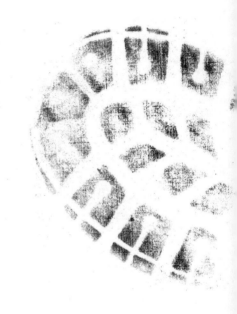

GROUP MESS

1. Create something here (a drawing, a word, a texture).
2. Ask a friend to add something to the page. (It's okay if it covers up your image.*)
3. Do something to alter what your friend did.
4. Repeat.

*Document the stages with photos if possible.

SMUDGE LOG

1. Create random smudges in each of these squares while you are going about your day. Experiment with different substances.
2. Document where and when each smudge was made.

DATE	DATE	DATE	DATE
TIME	TIME	TIME	TIME
LOCATION	LOCATION	LOCATION	LOCATION
DATE	DATE	DATE	DATE
TIME	TIME	TIME	TIME
LOCATION	LOCATION	LOCATION	LOCATION
DATE	DATE	DATE	DATE
TIME	TIME	TIME	TIME
LOCATION	LOCATION	LOCATION	LOCATION
DATE	DATE	DATE	DATE
TIME	TIME	TIME	TIME
LOCATION	LOCATION	LOCATION	LOCATION

DAMEN-BAD

photo credit: Arthur Dietrich, Seebad Heringsdorf u. Ostseebad Koserow

Delete or erase something.

1. Spill a substance here (some things that work well are coffee, tea, etc.). Let it dry.
2. Look for shapes in the dried substance, draw things based on what shapes you find (faces, characters, etc.).

1. Coat this page with paint.
2. Crumple up a piece of ordinary paper.
3. Drag the crumpled paper over the
   wet surface.

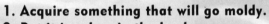

1. Acquire something that will go moldy.
2. Put it in a bag in the book.
(Note: not for the squeamish.)

YOU MUST SET ABOUT IT
MORE SLOWLY, ALMOST STUPIDLY
FORCE YOURSELF TO WRITE
DOWN WHAT IS OF NO
INTEREST, WHAT IS MOST
OBVIOUS, MOST COMMON,
MOST COLORLESS.

GEORGES . PEREC

FIELD TRIP: DOCUMENTATION

1. Go out into the world.
2. Find examples of various messes, spills, drips, accidents, grafitti.
3. Document them in some way.

Use this page as a palette. Mix colors, test brushstrokes, etc.

FURTHER
RESEARCH:

CHINESE
CALLIGRAPHY

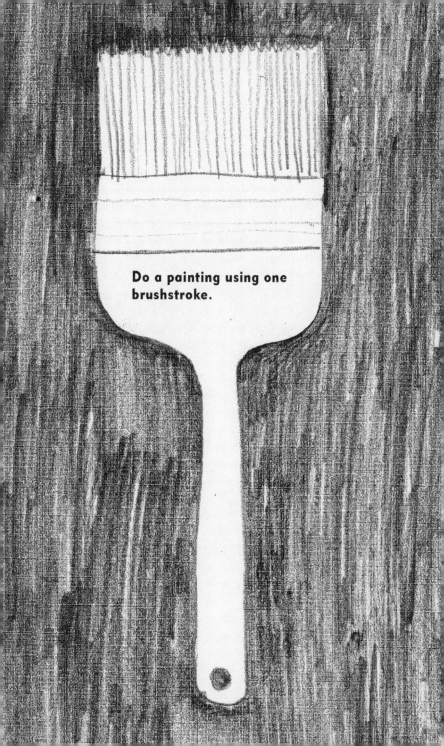

Do a painting using one brushstroke.

BLIND PHOTOGRAPHS

1. Point your camera without looking
   in the viewfinder.
2. Repeat. Take at least a dozen photos
   this way.

SCRIBBLE LOG

1. Create random scribbles in each of these squares while you are going about your day. Experiment with different utensils.
2. Document where and when each scribble was made.

DATE	**DATE**	**DATE**	**DATE**
TIME	**TIME**	**TIME**	**TIME**
LOCATION	**LOCATION**	**LOCATION**	**LOCATION**
DATE	**DATE**	**DATE**	**DATE**
TIME	**TIME**	**TIME**	**TIME**
LOCATION	**LOCATION**	**LOCATION**	**LOCATION**
DATE	**DATE**	**DATE**	**DATE**
TIME	**TIME**	**TIME**	**TIME**
LOCATION	**LOCATION**	**LOCATION**	**LOCATION**
DATE	**DATE**	**DATE**	**DATE**
TIME	**TIME**	**TIME**	**TIME**
LOCATION	**LOCATION**	**LOCATION**	**LOCATION**

Smear something here with your hands purely for the tactile sensation.

DAILY MESSES

–take a picture of your bed every morning
when you get out of it
–take a picture of your bedhead
–take a picture of your breakfast remnants

1. Think of an object.
2. Try to draw it by tearing.

Fill this page with things you can crumble.

1. Take the image to the right and cut it into pieces.
2. Rearrange the image to create a new image
   entirely.

FURTHER
RESEARCH:

R. BUCKMINSTER
FULLER

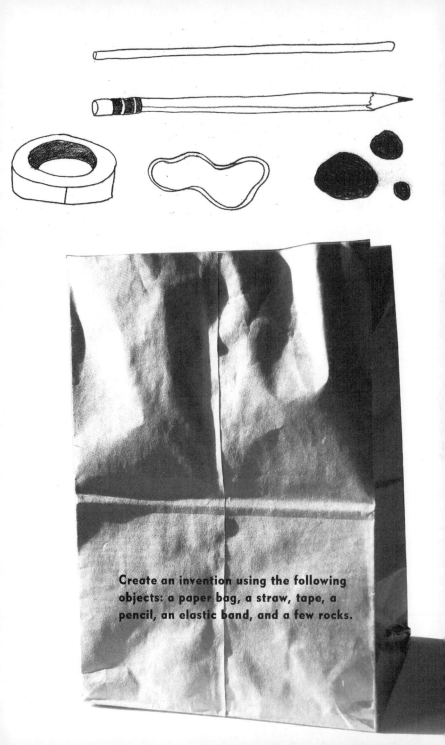

Create an invention using the following objects: a paper bag, a straw, tape, a pencil, an elastic band, and a few rocks.

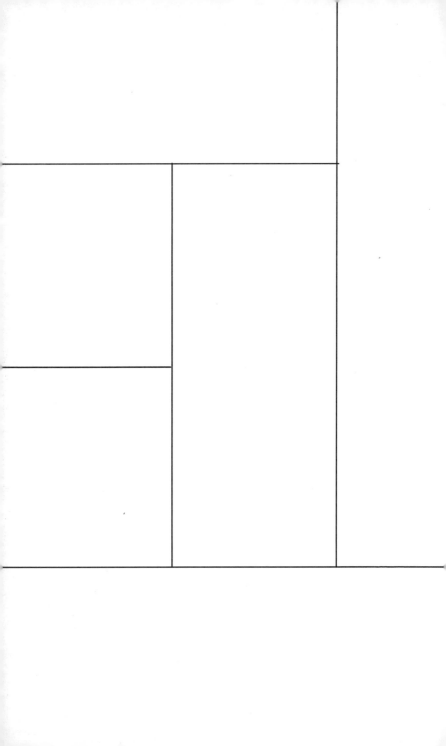

1. Do a pencil rubbing of a series of textures in the boxes (experiment with different materials).
2. Cut out random shapes.
3. Create a collage.

Do a drawing using only tape.

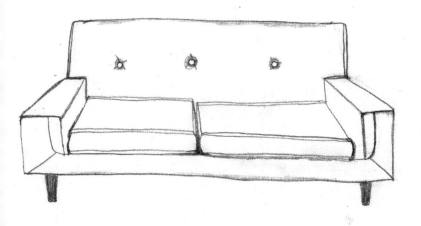

PSYCHOLOGICAL MESS

1. Get comfy.
2. Make a list of all your current problems.

Work with materials that bleed through the paper to the other side (markers, watercolor, pens). Create as much bleed as possible.

BLEED

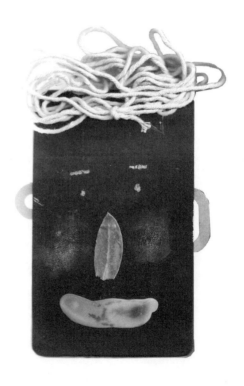

Create a face out of garbage and debris you find.

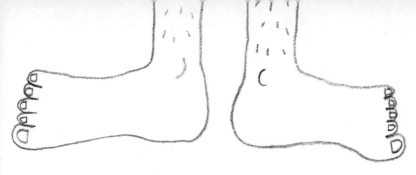

Write with your feet.

1. Cut out the instructions below.
2. Put them in a hat or bowl.
3. Pick them randomly to create a drawing.

DRAW AN EXPLOSION.	SCRIBBLE WILDLY.	DRAW TEN LINES.	CIRCLE IT.
DO NOTHING.	WRITE THE FIRST WORD YOU THINK OF.	FILL IN THE PAGE.	COLOR IT IN.
DRAW A MOUNTAIN.	DRAW SOMETHING RED.	DRAW A DOTTED LINE.	DRAW A HAT.
IT IS RAINING.	DRAW A BOX.	WRITE YOUR FIRST NAME.	DRAW A HEAD.
DRAW UPSIDE DOWN.	CONNECT THE CORNERS.	DRAW A CIRCLE.	DRAW A LINE.
ADD A PATTERN.	MAKE A HOLE.	COLOR IT IN.	DO IT AGAIN.
ADD SOME TAPE.	ADD STRIPES.	ADD SPOTS.	ERASE IT.
DRAW VERY LIGHTLY.	DRUM ON THE PAGE.	COVER IT UP.	USE A MARKER.
MAKE LARGE HEAVY STROKES.	MAKE A BUMPY LINE.	DRAW TEN TRIANGLES.	MAKE A FACE.

THOUGHT MESS

1. Hang many sheets of paper to your wall.
2. For one week write down your random thoughts
   on the wall.

1. Create a mess with mystery ingredients.
2. Have others try to guess what you used.

Layer this page with as many different materials as you can.

GROUP MESS

Challenge a friend to a mess duel.
Find a person to judge. The best
mess wins!

**Draw or paint with several utensils
(pens, pencils, pieces of chalk, etc.)
at once.**

Add 365 lines to this page.
(If you like you can do one a day for a year.)

1. Tie a piece of string to a pencil.
2. Dip the string into some kind of paint or ink.
3. Using the string as a whip, flail the string onto the paper.

DRAW A CIRCLE...

as if your pen just exploded.
as if your pen was on fire.
as if you had to kill time.
as if you had never drawn before.
as if there was a dog sitting on the middle of the page.
as if you had a terminal illness.
as if you were Picasso.
as if you were stranded on a desert island.
as a nose.
that is a symbol of impermanence.
that is a sun.
that looks like something else.
with corners.
that is a face.
that makes you laugh.
that flies.
you saw today.
from your dreams.
as a piece of furniture.
as a building.
as a sea monster.
that is hidden from view.
that is a portal.
that is life changing.
that scares you.
that has a soft texture.
that has a rough texture.
that makes a statement.
that is portable.
that conceals something.
that tells a story.
that moves.
that talks.
that you can consume.
that is heavy.
that is furry.
that is imaginary.

Do a drawing with a pin.

1. Fold page several times.
2. Make random cuttings with scissors.
3. Unfold.
4. Repeat with different folds.

1. Take an object you have multiples of. (Ideas: plastic bags, leaves, balloons, clothes, dirt.)
2. Create a huge mess by throwing the object randomly in the air.
3. Photograph it (or create a video).

How many things can you scrape here?

Write down what they are.

FURTHER RESEARCH:
WABI-SABI

FIELD TRIP: IMPERFECTION

Find several examples of a mess/
imperfection in nature.

Doodle by connecting the dots in an interesting way.

THE MINI ENCYCLOPEDIA

MOVEMENT			
MATERIALS			
WRITING			
SOCIAL INTERACTIONS			
MISC.			

OF MESSES AND MISTAKES

MOVEMENT			
MATERIALS			
WRITING			
SOCIAL INTERACTIONS			
MISC.			

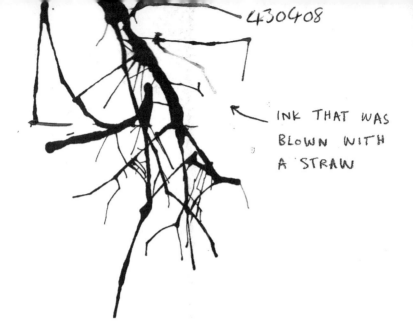

430408

INK THAT WAS
BLOWN WITH
A STRAW

ACKNOWLEDGMENTS

Some of the ideas in this book were influenced by an amazing (long out-of-print) book called *How to Design by Accident* by James F. O'Brien (Dover, 1968), which used a lot of heavy-duty artist materials in creating various textures. My versions rely only on healthy nontoxic materials, most of which you will already have on hand. Thanks also to my husband, Jefferson Pitcher, who once again worked as my model, and to my son, Tilden Pitcher, whose drawing was included in this book (a great artist at the age of two and king of messes). This book would not exist without the inspiring minds of my editor, Meg Leder, and publisher, John Duff, whose suggestions and comments always make my work better. And also to my agent, Faith Hamlin, whose constant support makes me feel completely blessed.

Washing Instructions
Hand wash or gentle cycle
on cold. Lay flat to dry.